PROBLEM PETS

PROBLEM PETS

Story and Photographs by
LILO HESS

Charles Scribner's Sons   New York

Easter is the herald of springtime, the season in which everything is fresh and new and nature begins again its cycle of life and growth. In cities and towns, store windows are decorated with pussy willows, bright jonquils, gay Easter eggs, chocolate bunnies, and sugar or marshmallow chicks and ducks.

But in some store windows we see live baby rabbits and live fluffy yellow chicks and ducklings. They are only a few days old and huddle together for warmth. It is hard to resist the urge to cuddle them, and since they are inexpensive, many people buy them as toys or novelties for their small children. As soon as they get them home, the problem begins. Where should they be kept? What should they be fed? How can one keep the pet dog or cat away from them? Since they are so young and delicate, most of them have already caught colds in the drafty store windows. How can they be cured? Most of the little chicks and ducklings survive only a few hours or days in their new homes. Some get stepped on; some get squeezed, frightened, or neglected.

Baby chicks and ducklings need warmth and quiet to survive. Just a warm room is not enough; they need to be brooded. In nature the mother hen or duck sits on them to keep them warm, and they emerge from under her feathers only to feed and drink. In the home, a low-watt bulb (about fifteen or twenty-five watts) set in an aluminum reflector under which they can huddle will keep the babies warm. It is best to keep them in a box that is roomy enough for them to run around in; their droppings are very messy, and they have a knack for getting into trouble if allowed to run free. A baby duck might take a bath in the coffee cup or drink milk from it, or it might upset a box containing soap powder or nibble the freshly baked cake.

Chick starter feed can be bought at most pet stores and all feed stores, and both chicks and ducklings will eat it. Later, the chicks get scratch feed and the ducklings a special pellet. They need fresh water at all times.

After the ducklings are a few weeks old, they might enjoy a brief swim in the bathtub. Their owner must watch at first to make sure that they don't drown.

When feathers start to replace the soft fluffy down, the chicks and ducklings look awkward and scrawny, and most people lose interest in them. Unless one knows a farmer or a friend with a country home who will take them, there is seldom someone who will adopt them. They cannot be released to run

wild, since most domesticated animals have long lost the ability to fend for themselves. So no matter how dear those Easter chicks and ducklings are, they should not be bought by people who cannot care for them after they are grown up.

The little Easter bunnies are much hardier and easier to keep than the chicks and ducklings. If possible rabbits should be kept in a yard or garden. A cage made of wire or a large crate equipped with a wire front and a door will make a fine home. Place a warm, straw-lined sleeping box inside. Commercially sold rabbit pellets with additional carrots, lettuce, dandelion greens, apples, or similar roughage, as well as fresh water, are all a rabbit seems to need to stay healthy.

All through the ages man has cherished and cultivated the companionship of animals. There is scarcely an animal known that has not been kept as a pet by someone at some time.

Few people would consider keeping a walrus, shark, tiger, or elephant as a pet around the house, yet these animals could be kept if they were given the right kind of place in which to live, in the right climate, with the right food and care. But no matter how good-natured and well-trained an elephant is, it just won't fit into an apartment or private home. Just like baby chicks and ducklings, the elephant is not a suitable household pet.

But what about the little helpless fawn lying under a bush or in the tall grass? It seems to be alone and abandoned. Or the nest full of wild rabbits which are probably orphaned, since there is no mother to be seen? Wouldn't those animals make unusual and loving pets?

Every spring, when people hike or drive in the country, wild baby animals are found. Some are even sold in pet stores or by animal dealers. The temptation to pick up these animals or to buy them and take them home is very strong in most of us. But very few of them make good pets after they are grown, which is usually in only a few weeks or months, depending on the species.

Unless you know for certain that an animal has lost its mother through an accident, don't assume the "lonely baby" is abandoned. The mother is always nearby, watching from a secret hiding place. In the case of foxes, wolves, wild cats of various kinds, most birds, and some other animals, even the father shares in the care of the young after they have been weaned. Only if both parents are killed are the babies in need of human help. Usually it is best to take just a quick look at any wild baby one sees and then, without touching or disturbing the nest, walk away.

If it really is necessary to care for a young orphaned animal, the local game warden or conservation department must be consulted, since many states have strict laws about picking up and keeping wild animals.

All baby mammals must be bottle-fed until they can eat by themselves. If they are very small, they should be fed a formula of one part evaporated milk mixed with two parts water.

Weight of animal in ounces	Tablespoons of evaporated milk per day
2	1½
4	2
6	3
8	4
12	5

Do not force a baby animal to eat more than it wants, but make sure each gets its share. One way of telling if a baby has had enough to eat is to look at its tummy, which will get

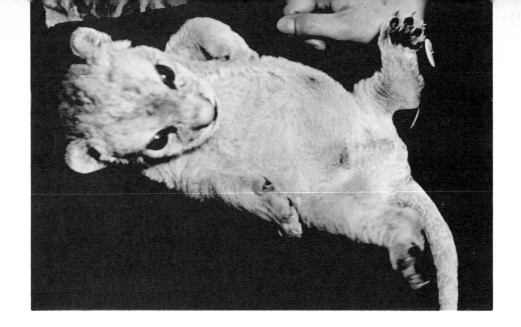

rounded and full as it nurses. A few drops of multiple vitamins should be added to each formula. Some wild babies prefer their milk a little sweetened and for them Karo syrup can be added—a few drops for tiny ones, a teaspoonful for larger animals. The formula must be lukewarm and new-born mammals must be fed every two hours, day and night. Larger babies, such as fawns or bear cubs, can be fed about four times a day. Some babies are so small that one has to feed them with an eyedropper or a doll's bottle till their mouths are large enough to take a regular baby bottle.

When the babies are about three to four weeks old, they can be given their evaporated milk mixed one part milk to one part water. After about five weeks they can be slowly accustomed to taking regular cow's milk. At that time pablum should be added to the milk to give it more substance. The meat eaters can be taught to lap milk mixed with a little chopped meat out of a dish. Animals that eat plants or grain usually can chew at an earlier age and can be fed some of their natural foods while still on the bottle. Offering the babies some solid foods is a way to tell when they are ready to be weaned.

Baby animals have to be kept warm at all times. An electric heating pad, its thermostat set at "low," wrapped in woolen material or in a Turkish towel, should be placed so that it covers half of the box in which the animals are kept. The little babies can then crawl off the pad if they get too hot.

Baby raccoons are probably the most popular and most delightful wild animal pets. They are playful, mischievous, clever, and full of curiosity and affection. But if they are given the run of the house, their owners must be prepared to live in continuous turmoil and to have the place in a shambles. If raccoons are to be caged outdoors, they must have plenty of room. Strong wire, even on the bottom of the cage, is necessary. A good lock on the door is also a must; otherwise, just like monkeys, they will figure out a way to open it sooner or later. The cage should contain a few logs and a tree for climbing. A sturdy hardwood tree with its top and small branches removed will be best. Raccoons also need a comfortable sleeping box lined with straw, hay, or dry leaves. In addition to the

drinking water, a large pan of water for bathing, washing, and dunking should be provided. The food-washing ceremony for which they are so famous is greatly exaggerated. Raccoons do not wash their food to clean it, and they will eat even if no water is available, but they do like to dunk and moisten their food if they can.

An adult raccoon should be fed twice a day. In the morning it can be fed carrots, celery, raw or cooked potatoes, apples, and other fruits in season. In the evening it should get raw chopped meat or dog food with some cod-liver oil and bone meal added. A pet raccoon should be inoculated against distemper.

Unfortunately most raccoons lose their pleasing dispositions when they become mature, and many become aggressive and unpredictable and resent being penned up. Some people tether raccoons and other wild creatures and never allow them any freedom. This is a very cruel practice. The unfortunate animals just pace back and forth, never able to display their natural grace and dignity, and usually become very mean.

It is best to release an adopted raccoon as soon as possible. Late summer is a good time because there is still plenty of food available. The release should be gradual. That means the animal should be allowed to roam outdoors but still receive additional food until it can fend for itself.

No animal that has been a pet in the home should ever be released in the fall or winter. Raccoons, bears, porcupines, deer, squirrels, rabbits, chipmunks and other rodents are some of the animals that seem to be able to readjust to life in the wild after having been kept as temporary pets. Animals that have to learn from their parents how to hunt and stalk prey, such as foxes, wild cats, or wolves, can never be released because they lack this skill.

Sometimes a baby porcupine is found after its mother has been killed on the highway or in some other accident. This prickly baby becomes very tame, but it is stubborn and far from an ideal house companion. If kept in a cage, it usually becomes lonesome and melancholy and cries a great deal. If given the run of the house, it will gnaw on almost every piece of wood it sees; table and chair legs seem to be favorites. Contrary to popular belief, the porcupine's quills are not "shot out" but have hooked barbs that stick to any part of a human or animal that touches them. The barbs are difficult and painful to remove. A baby porcupine should never be handled without heavy gloves, no matter how friendly it is.

The name porcupine comes from two Latin words, *porcus,* meaning "pig," and *spina,* meaning "spines" or "thorns." When the animal is aroused the quills are raised, making a very effective defense against almost all enemies. Since almost

16

no animal can harm the porcupine, it seems to take life very placidly, ambling along on the ground or climbing leisurely among the branches of its favorite food trees. The North American porcupine eats bark, leaves, and the new growth of evergreen trees.

After the baby porcupine has been weaned, it should be taught to eat those natural foods, supplemented with apples, carrots, and some grain. Then it should be released as soon as possible in a secluded place near evergreen trees and water.

One wild animal baby that is never found alone in a nest or under a bush is the opossum. Like a kangaroo, the opossum mother carries her young ones in a fur-lined pouch. The opossum is the only pouched mammal, or marsupial, in the United States. When the young become too large for the pouch they cling to their mother's back and sides.

Many opossums are killed yearly on the highway, and sometimes a baby survives the accident, in which case it should be taken home and cared for. If one finds a young adult it is best to put it right back into the woods, for an opossum is not the kind of animal that makes a good pet.

Playfulness and inquisitiveness in animals is a sign of intelligence, but the young opossum plays very little. It is often hostile and unhappy in captivity and can bite very hard. It is interesting in many ways though. It has a prehensile tail which it uses to hang and climb with. It has more teeth than other animals, fifty in all, and its defense of rolling over as if it were dead, "playing 'possum," is well known.

The opossum grows as large as a house cat and is not very clean. As soon as a baby opossum has its teeth, it can be fed raw chopped meat or dog food, milk with coddled egg, and a variety of fruits and vegetables. Individual opossums have different tastes and preferences and soon let their owner know what they like. The cage or box should be lined with absorbent material, such as shredded paper or wood shavings, and some branches for climbing should be provided. Then, as soon as possible, the animal should be set free.

Unfortunately, most states have "open season" on foxes. That means they can be hunted and killed at any time of the year, even in the spring when they have young ones in the den. If the vixen, the female fox, is killed while her pups are still nursing they cannot survive. If they are old enough to eat solid food, the male fox can take care of them. If both parents are dead or the pups are still nursing when the mother is killed, they should be taken home and cared for. Baby foxes make very cute pets. Playful and friendly like puppies, they get along well with other household pets, and many can be housebroken. They should be inoculated against distemper and kept warm and dry and given a lot of attention. As soon as they are weaned they should be fed raw chopped meat, dog food, and some fruit. Poultry parts and an occasional mouse should be included in their diet as well as vitamins and cod-liver oil. Since foxes have a musky odor it is best to house them outdoors when they are about three or four months old.

A single animal might get very lonesome so, if possible, foxes should be kept in pairs. These active and intelligent

animals must have a chance to play and explore in the home as well as outdoors. Balls to roll, hollow logs to run through and play tag on, large bones to chew, soil to dig in, and stones to turn over will help to keep them entertained. They can also be trained to walk on a leash. If they are used to the home they usually stay close by and can be let out to play. Their cage must be very roomy, and the bottom should have wire mesh; otherwise they will dig their way out. Since they had no parents to teach them how to hunt and take care of themselves, someone must look after them all of their lives. Zoos or game refuges, which are always short of space and have more than enough foxes, will seldom take them. So unless it is absolutely necessary, don't pick up baby foxes. Besides, most of them become unmanageable for the average person when they are fully grown and have to be caged for the rest of their lives.

Every spring, fawns are found and taken home as pets, regardless of the laws that prohibit it. Only if a nursing doe is killed or if one finds an injured fawn should those graceful babies be taken from their natural environment. In each case the local authorities must be notified and a temporary permit obtained that allows the possession of a wild creature.

A little fawn is usually easy to take care of. It needs a warm place to sleep; a room such as a kitchen or warm bathroom might do. One must be careful that the fawn does not slip on a waxed or tiled floor since its legs are very thin and delicate and break easily. A fawn quickly makes friends with other animals in the home and will follow its owner about like a puppy. If one lives in the country it will stay around the house that has become home and go along on walks. The fawn usually can be fed a formula of evaporated milk mixed with an equal amount of water right from the start. It can drink right away from a regular baby bottle, four feedings per day of six to eight ounces of formula, depending on its size. It will also nibble on hay or grass very soon, and some should be given to it from the start. When it is about five weeks old, grain or pellets should be fed. It also likes potato peelings and pieces of apple and carrot.

An older fawn should be kept in a cage with high, strong wire sides so that it cannot jump over it. Eight feet is a mini-

mum height. The cage should be large enough for the deer to exercise in, at least twelve feet long.

Once a deer has become a pet releasing it is difficult. Not only is it very attached to its owner, but it has lost all fear of man and therefore is easy game for trigger-happy hunters. Moreover, it will have a hard time establishing itself in the wild, since other deer usually do not tolerate a newcomer in their territory.

It is very difficult for people to realize that the gentle little fawn that was such a loving and helpless pet will often turn into a treacherous and dangerous animal when adult. Bucks especially are prone to turn on their owners and inflict serious injuries. A doe usually stays more placid. Anyone adopting a fawn should be fully aware of the responsibilities and difficulties that lie ahead.

Although otters live over almost all of the United States, except in dry regions, not many young ones are orphaned. If one should find an otter pup that needs to be cared for, a permit is needed to keep it. Otters perform delightful clownish antics and make good part-time pets for people living in the country. City people should never attempt to raise otters.

Some otters live near rivers. They feed on crayfish, frogs, fish, turtles, and salamanders and might also eat small rabbits or water fowl. In captivity otters can be given raw chopped meat and dog meal mixed together. But they also need fish several times a week. Small babies should be bottle-fed with the evaporated-milk formula and kept warm and dry.

Otter pups develop a little slower than most other mammal babies. Their eyes do not open until they are four or five weeks old. After they have been weaned, they don't seem to like milk anymore and should have fresh water, preferably from a small flow. They need a comfortable nest box and can be trained to use a special place for their toilet. They also need a fresh-water pool, pond, river, or even a large tank or bathtub in which to swim and dive. They can be taken out on a leash, and they will form close friendships with the family cat or dog.

They like to play with balls, slide down grassy slopes, or

retrieve sticks. As soon as possible they should be released into their natural environment. But first they must be taught to catch fish and other natural food. If they are allowed to root in the soft mud of river banks or ponds and encouraged through praise to chase after fish, these highly intelligent animals will soon learn to take care of themselves.

One of the few wild babies that remains quite tame during its adult life, if treated kindly, is the skunk. Orphaned babies can be raised easily on the evaporated-milk formula, but as soon as they can eat solids, they should get chopped meat, dog food, and various fruits and vegetables. When raised in the home with a family they adapt themselves easily to human ways. Since they are not too inquisitive or lively they can be kept in an apartment. If a box filled with sand or cat litter is kept near their sleeping quarters, they soon learn to use it.

The glands which give forth the strong odor for which skunks are famous can be removed by a veterinarian in a fairly simple operation when the animals are about six or eight weeks old. Once its special weapon of defense is gone, however, the skunk can never be released. Before adopting a little skunk and having it de-scented, its owner must be very sure that he or she is willing to provide a good home for this animal for many years to come.

If possible, the skunk should be kept out-of-doors. Its cage should be dry and roomy and have a wire bottom, since the skunk can dig and would eventually find a way to escape. It needs a sleeping box or a hollow log with hay or straw bedding. The skunk is more active by night, but in time it can be trained to feed and move about in the daytime.

Flying squirrels live in many parts of the United States, and yet few people ever see them because they are shy and move about only at night. But in the spring, baby flying squirrels are sometimes found after a storm has broken the branch in which they had their nest or when the tree that was their home has been cut down. Usually the mother will move them immediately to a new, safe place. They should not be touched unless the mother does not pick them up or unless some of the babies have been injured in the fall. If only one baby is hurt, it might be advisable to take a second, healthy one along for companionship. These little squirrels are happier and do better in captivity when they are not alone.

The babies should be fed evaporated-milk formula out of a doll's bottle until their teeth appear; then they will crack and eat sunflower seeds, small grains, and peanuts. Harder nuts must be cracked for them, but they can remove the meat inside for themselves. Pieces of orange and apple, lettuce, and grapes, as well as some dry bread, should be fed about three or four times a week. Mealworms or tiny pieces of meat should also be fed from time to time, and supplementary vitamins must be given.

Flying squirrels will live quite well in a small cage, provided they are let out to run and exercise daily. If confined to cramped quarters for any length of time, they will tend, like all caged animals, to get "cage paralysis" in their hind legs, which is very difficult to cure.

Flying squirrels must have natural branches of various thicknesses in their cage, not only to exercise on but also to gnaw on. Like all rodents, they must file down their chisel teeth through gnawing to keep them in good shape. They need a warm nest box to sleep in and will soon learn to come out for food and play during the daytime.

These pretty fawn-colored animals with white underparts and large dark eyes do not really fly but glide from taller trees or branches to lower ones. A furred membrane, which connects their front and hind legs, is stretched out for their glides, and the flat tail helps to balance them. Never hold or pull a flying squirrel by the tail, since the fur will slide off the bone like a glove and will never grow back, thus preventing the animal from leaping and gliding properly. Though the young make fairly good pets, it is best to return them to their natural habitat as soon as they are able to care for themselves. Adult squirrels seldom become very tame.

Spring is also the time when people find baby birds that have either fallen out of the nest or are injured or orphaned. Only in such cases should a human lend a helping hand. Never take a bird out of a nest just to keep it as a pet. Many birds are hard to raise because of their highly specialized diets. If a baby bird must be taken care of, it should be put gently into a makeshift nest. The nest can be a commercial one or one made out of dry grass, soft hay, shredded facial tissues, or even an old woolen sock. It is advisable to dust the nest with lice and mite powder, the kind sold for cage birds, before the bird is put into the nest. The nest should be put into the corner of a box or cage in such a way as to prevent the baby from falling out and from being vulnerable to other household pets.

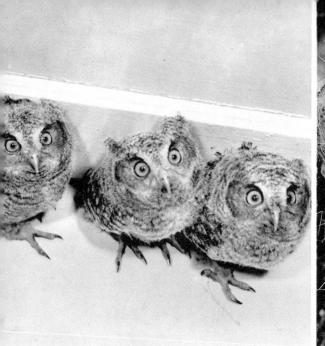

After one has determined what kind of bird one has adopted and what its natural foods are, a diet must be worked out that is as close as possible to its natural requirements. For the very young, small bird, whether seed or insect eater, a starting diet can be made from mixing hard-boiled egg yoke and un-sweetened biscuit or pablum with a little water to make a paste. Insect eaters can soon be given a little chopped, lean, raw meat or, better, chopped earthworms and small soft-bodied flies. Larger meat eaters, such as owls, hawks, and vultures, can be given pieces of dog food or raw meat and, a little later, poultry parts and if possible some mice.

Very small birds need to eat a little every hour but usually do not have to be fed at night. As long as the food is moistened they need no extra water until they eat seeds; then they must have fresh water to drink. As soon as possible birds should be taught to pick up food from the hand or from the bottom of the cage. Then, when they are able to eat by themselves and have learned to fly, they should be released.

Some birds, such as crows, will remain very attached to their keepers, and many stay close to their foster homes even after they have been released and can care for themselves. Others often return with a mate and stay to nest and raise their family near their human friends.

Crows and grackles are two of the few birds that require no permit to keep in most states and make good pets. Crows are often shrewd pickpockets, making off with objects that take their fancy, such as coins or jewelry, and hiding them. They can be taught to talk. If allowed to fly outside, they will return to their cage and home.

Frogs, toads, turtles, snakes, lizards, and salamanders are often part-time or permanent guests in a home. They present no problems as pets and therefore will not be discussed here. But some of those animals, if picked up in the wild, will be very unhappy in captivity and refuse to eat. They must be "force-fed" for a while; then, if after a few weeks they still refuse to eat and adjust, they should be released in or near the place where they were captured. Some turtles and snakes are protected by law and cannot be kept without a permit.

Baby bears are sometimes found orphaned in the wild. But sometimes people buy them from roadside zoos or from dealers.

33

Black bears are more numerous in the western part of the
United States than in the east. Unless one is an experienced
animal handler one should never attempt to raise and keep a
bear cub, no matter how cute the little fellow is. Never go near
a bear cub in the woods, even if it seems to be alone. The
mother is very protective, always nearby, and she will attack
anyone who comes near her cubs.

There are usually two to four cubs born in January or Feb-
ruary while the mother is still in her winter den, a cave or
other sheltered place. The tiny bears weigh only from nine to

fifteen ounces, have very thin fur, and their eyes are closed. By the time the mother is ready to emerge from her winter quarters, the cubs are three to four months old and ready to go with her on outings and to play.

If a bear cub must be taken care of for a short time, it can be fed lukewarm formula of one part evaporated milk and one part water from a baby bottle. It usually takes about eight ounces per feeding and should get fed every two hours. If it is very small a heating pad should be provided. A cub that is able to chew can be given bread soaked in milk, cut-up apples, meat scraps, and some dog food.

A bear cub is full of fun and mischief. If it has the run of the house the cub will make the most of it and enjoy itself tremendously, but its foster parents might not appreciate the fun. Everything edible is eaten, and everything movable is turned over. The cub will follow its owner about and can be taken out for walks without a leash. If something alarms it, the cub will seek refuge in a tree until the danger is past. But soon it grows more independent and stubborn and cannot be trusted. It longs to be free but cannot be returned to the wild since it has lost its fear of humans and has failed to develop its natural instincts. Usually the bear's fate is confinement in a miserable roadside zoo or traveling circus. Few good zoos have room to take extra bears.

Wolves are so scarce in the United States, after years of persecution and slaughter, that they are now on the list of wildlife in danger of extinction and are protected in many states by law. Wolves are very powerful animals with large teeth and thick, beautiful fur. They are much more high-strung and active than dogs and are definitely not house pets. Although they can learn to walk on the leash, sit, lie down, or come on command, their obedience is not a blind subservient action and cannot always be depended on. Their loyalty to men is of an uncertain quality.

In the spring of every year wolf pups are sold by dealers and shipped all over the United States. The price is about two hundred dollars apiece. The ancestors of these pups may have been raised in captivity for many generations, but they are still classified as wild animals, and it is against the law in most states to own one. If the authorities hear of a person owning a wolf, they will confiscate it, no matter how tame and well cared for the animal is. And if a wolf pup that has been raised with love is separated from its home and owner it will lose its spirit and often will not survive.

An orphaned or injured wolf pup which must be given a temporary home can be kept by obtaining a temporary permit under the "wildlife in distress" law, which most states have adopted.

Very young pups should be fed the evaporated-milk formula, according to their weight, about four times a day. When they are fully grown, they eat about three pounds of horse-meat and a half pound of dog meal mixed with some bone meal daily.

If a wolf is permanently injured and its owner allowed to keep it, the animal should be inoculated against dog distemper. Its cage must be large, about ten feet wide and twenty-five feet long, to give the wolf enough space to exercise.

People living in the western United States often keep coyotes as pets. Either orphaned pups are taken from the den, after the parents have been accidentally—or deliberately—killed, or young individuals that have strayed to a ranch in search of food are captured and raised. Feelings run high whenever the coyote is mentioned. Some people believe that the only good coyote is a dead one; others, including wildlife organizations, want to preserve the coyote as part of our wilderness heritage. It is hard to believe, in the light of all the research showing that predators are important in maintaining the balance of nature, that some states still pay bounty (that is, a reward) for every dead coyote. Other states have open season on the animal, which means it can be killed anytime, even when it has young in its den. Many states are now trying to persuade people to save the coyote, demonstrating that the coyote does more good

by eating the rodents and insects that destroy crops than harm by eating an occasional lamb or chicken.

Coyotes have slanting eyes and an eerie howl. They also bark, yip, and grunt. They often interbreed with dogs, and this mixture, the coy-dog, is preferred by many ranches to regular dogs.

A litter of two to nine coyote pups is born in the spring, and both parents help to feed and train them. In the fall the young strike out on their own. The care and food of the coyote pup in captivity is the same as that for the wolf. Only people living in wide-open country, which is the natural home of the coyote, should ever try to keep one. All other pet coyotes usually end up behind bars in a zoo.

An animal's life in nature consists of searching for food, finding suitable shelter, avoiding enemies, mating, and raising a family. In captivity all these activities and drives become unnecessary. Deprived of all its natural ways of occupying itself, a captive animal usually becomes listless and bored. It might also refuse to eat. Without the will to live, wild creatures quickly become prone to all kinds of illnesses, especially lung disorders. Many die or need costly veterinary care.

Making an animal happy and content is just as important as giving it food and water. This can be done by giving it an interest in life, something to do, to play with, to explore, as well as companionship, either human or animal. A pet is happy when it has an environment closely resembling the one it has come from, and when it can live, eat, breed, and play in a natural way.

A human's relationship with a wild animal is often more intimate and rewarding than one with a domesticated pet. Domesticated animals are usually eager to please their masters, while a wild creature is more aloof and reserved. It is an achievement if the wild pet bestows its affection and trust on its owner, a trust that should never be betrayed.

In recent years it has become more and more fashionable to keep exotic animals as pets. Hundreds of thousands of wild animals are imported yearly into the United States for the pet trade.

Almost all the animals that are imported are delicate babies. Before they even reach their destinations, about seventy-five percent die of neglect, disease, or from being kept in cramped quarters, as well as from anguish and lonesomeness. More are lost in pet shops and at wholesale dealers. People who buy those "cute babies" usually get already weakened, sick, drugged, and unhappy specimens that need extensive medical treatment from the start. The enthusiasm that makes a person get an exotic animal in the first place soon fades, and the creature becomes a tremendous burden.

Most wild animals, if they are healthy, will tear the house apart unless they are confined. They cannot be taken on trips or put into kennels. Friends wrinkle their noses at the "strange odor" in the house, since very few animals can be housebroken, and are often afraid of being attacked. Even the owners are not always safe from the claws or fangs of their difficult wild houseguests. A family's entire life must change to revolve around an exotic pet.

Housing the animal is, of course, the main consideration. If someone asks why spend a hundred dollars on a cage for an

animal that costs only twenty-five, it shows that the person has no knowledge of or feeling for the needs of animals. Such a person should never be allowed to keep a living creature. Almost all major zoos now have recognized the mental and physical misery animals endure through boredom and lack of space, and are making great efforts to provide better living conditions for their charges. Happier animals make better shows. The same goes for the pet in the home. Never get an animal, no matter how small or inexpensive it might be, if you cannot provide roomy quarters, the right kind of food, attention, companionship, and diversion for it.

Many people are great cat lovers and want to go further with this hobby than keeping the domestic kinds. They try to keep the "big cats" as house companions but soon find that this is an almost impossible task. If kittens are found hurt or orphaned in the wild, they should be regarded as very temporary guests only, and none should be bought in pet shops. No matter how lovable the wild kittens are, few can be handled when they are adult. They turn quickly from playing to biting and scratching, and many become so powerful that even playful antics could be dangerous.

African lion cubs are often seen for sale in pet shops. Most of them are a sorry sight, rickety, undernourished, weak, and unhappy. People often buy them out of pity. If they can be nursed back to health, they are cuddly, gentle, and playful, and their owners have fun with them for a few months; then, nothing but trouble and sorrow. They find that no zoo wants to take their pet, since lions are easily bred in captivity, and most zoos have more than they want. If the animal can be placed in a roadside zoo or carnival, they stay barely alive in cramped, dirty quarters and are often harassed, teased, and mistreated.

All wild cats when very young should first be given the evaporated-milk formula fortified with multiple vitamins and a pinch of dicalcium phosphate. They can be given about two ounces of formula every two hours, increasing the amount ac-

cording to their weight. When the kittens are about five weeks old a little meat juice can be added; at eight weeks, small balls of chopped raw meat can be fed. As soon as they have teeth, they can be switched to an all-meat diet, with some additional bones to chew on. Milk can be lapped from a dish if the animal still will take it.

There is a smaller cat, native to the area from the southwestern United States to Argentina, that is a great favorite with exotic-cat fanciers. This is the pretty ocelot, a slender animal with yellowish-brown fur and various sized black spots that form stripes along its sides and neck. When fully grown an ocelot may weigh thirty to thirty-five pounds. Ocelot owners have organized clubs throughout the United States, where they get together and exchange experiences and seek advice from one another.

There are many different opinions as to the question, Does the ocelot make a good household pet? Some owners claim that ocelots stay very tame and get along well with other family members and pets, and tell of the few cases where they have even bred in captivity. Other owners report unfortunate experiences. Their pet has turned on them or on their friends and has become untrustworthy and unmanageable. However, all owners seem to agree on one point: you don't own an ocelot, it owns you.

Although the ocelot has not yet become extinct, its numbers in the wild have dropped sharply, and it is now on the list of endangered species. For every kitten that is imported alive, seven have died, and many adults are still killed for their fur.

An ocelot that is captive in a private home usually does not live long. It may die of disease or accident, or its owner may have to dispose of it because its wild temperament does not conform to the human way of life.

A close cousin of the ocelot, and often confused with it or even sold as an ocelot, is the smaller, daintier margay cat, which is native from southern Texas to northern Uruguay. These two cats are very similar in their way of life, food, character, and general appearance. Small kittens must be kept warm and dry in a box with a heating pad wrapped in toweling. To their milk formula, multiple vitamins must be added, and when they are older and weaned, some bone meal or calcium as well as cod-liver oil should be given. In nature they catch rats, mice, rabbits, and other small mammals, as well as some birds. In captivity they need raw meat and poultry parts. To provide the roughage that most meat eaters need, mice should be fed from time to time, and the poultry parts should be fed with the feathers still on.

A wild cat should be vaccinated against feline distemper and enteritis. If it lives in a cage, the cat must have logs to sharpen its claws on, shelves to sleep on, and toys with which to amuse

itself. It can be trained to walk on a leash or chain, and most of them can be housebroken.

Most states require that the owners of wild cats obtain special permits from the game or health departments. It might also be advisable for owners of the big cats to take out special insurance, because even a friendly animal might jump up on a visitor and scratch him or tear his clothing.

People who don't quite dare to get one of the larger cats but like an animal that looks and acts a little like a feline sometimes buy a genet. The genet does not belong to the cat family; it is related to the mongoose. Its habitat is Africa, Asia, and southern Europe. It is a very graceful, bright-eyed little creature with a pointed nose. It is yellowish-brown with dark brown or black spots and a ringed tail. When very young the genet makes a charming pet. It is playful and affectionate. It learns to walk on a leash and can be toilet-trained. Its diet is the same as that of the ocelot and margay, allowing for its smaller size.

In ancient Egypt genets were tamed and trained to catch mice. But when the genet matures, its fierce nature becomes more apparent and allowing it to roam freely in a home would not be safe. Genets are mostly night animals and tree climbers. Their cage should be at least six to eight feet high, six feet long and about four feet wide. It must contain branches strong enough for climbing and jumping and a sleeping box well off

the ground. In colder climates the genet needs heated quarters.

Two animals related to the raccoon have recently become extremely popular pets. They are the coatimundi and the kinkajou. They are sold for about thirty dollars in most pet shops. Naturally, at the time of sale they are babies or young adults and very gentle. Some pet stores even give them tranquilizers to make them easier to handle. Though they are not the most difficult animals to keep, they do require specialized care and lots of attention. Not all remain trustworthy when fully grown.

The kinkajou, or honeybear, comes from Central America. It has a prehensile tail like some monkeys and is altogether somewhat monkeylike in its ways. Unlike its relative the raccoon, it has no rings on its tail. Its fur is short and thick, mostly honey colored, although a few individuals are almost gray or even chocolate brown. The kinkajou has soft, dark, expressive eyes. In nature it is nocturnal, living in trees and feeding on insects, fruits and berries, and probably some birds' eggs.

In captivity the kinkajou is full of fun and mischief. It quickly learns to take advantage of a lenient owner by lolling on the bed, relaxing in the sink, swinging from lamps, or demanding milk from a bottle long after it has been weaned. However, it can attack and bite when something does not go its way, hanging tight with its feet and prehensile tail, making itself hard to shake off.

The kinkajou's diet in captivity should consist of raw or cooked meat, raw eggs, bone meal, bread, apples, grapes, bananas, and oranges. Ice cream is a treat all kinkajous seem to love. They should also be inoculated against distemper.

The kinkajou needs to be kept warm and therefore requires an indoor cage during cold weather. The cage must be large enough to accommodate branches for climbing and a sleeping platform. A hollow log about sixteen to twenty inches high, standing on end, might also serve as a retreat. This animal is long-lived. One kept at the zoo in Amsterdam, Holland, lived over twenty-three years, but the average age limit in captivity is between ten and fifteen years. So if you want to adopt a kinkajou, you must be willing to care for it a long time.

In the pet section of metropolitan newspapers we may often see an advertisement offering for adoption a "lovable" coatimundi, stating that its owner can no longer care for it. On closer investigation, it usually turns out that the animal has bitten someone. As with all other mammals, the coatimundi is a fine pet when young but usually changes in later life, although some of them will remain fairly friendly if treated well.

The coatis most often sold come from the Mexican border of the United States and from South America. Their color is grayish-brown, with lighter faces and a clearly ringed tail. They have a very long nose that can be bent up or down or sideways,

almost like a miniature elephant's-trunk. There are several species of coatis. In nature they poke their long noses into tree cavities, holes in the ground, or under rocks in their continuous search for something edible. They eat insects, small birds or mammals, and various kinds of fruits and berries.

They are usually healthy, but it might be advisable to give them a bath to get rid of fleas or other parasites. They probably will object to this with loud squeals, but the young seldom bite. Their cage must be especially reinforced on top and bottom since they are good climbers as well as diggers. Branches and a sleeping box should be in the cage, and they should be

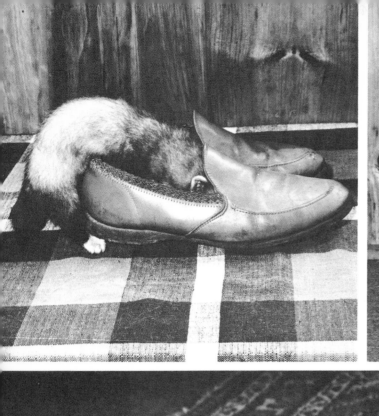

given hollow logs, balls, and other toys to play with. As long as they are young and friendly they can be kept in the house and walked on a leash.

People who live near the coati's natural habitat and pick up orphaned babies should release them as soon as they can care for themselves. Coatis that have been purchased in a store must be cared for all of their lives, probably about ten years. Their diet is the same as that of the raccoon. They should also be inoculated against distemper.

From time to time, a ferret, a small weasel-like animal from Europe, is offered for sale in pet stores. Many states prohibit keeping this animal as a pet although it is often kept in Europe. The European ferret has a good disposition if it is handled often, and it remains friendly and playful even after it matures. Only during the mating season or if there are young ones in the nest will it become difficult to approach. Since it is easily bred in captivity, it is best to keep male and female separate. Ferrets also quarrel often among themselves.

In Europe ferrets were bred especially for hunting rabbits. Their long, slim bodies and their very short legs were well suited to slithering down rabbit holes. At one time ferrets were used in the United States to exterminate mice and rats, and no cat ever cleaned a cellar or barn out as quickly as a ferret. Unfortunately, ferrets also kill chickens, pheasants, and rabbits, which is why they are not allowed as pets in some parts of the country.

The black-footed ferret, native to the western United States, has become almost extinct. It lives in prairie-dog villages and dines on the prairie dog, but now that man has destroyed most of the prairie-dog towns, the black-footed ferret has almost vanished.

The ferret has a very strong odor and therefore cannot be kept indoors for long. An outdoor cage, with a wire bottom to facilitate cleaning, should be about six feet long and four feet wide. It does not have to be very high, since ferrets do not climb. The ferret needs a sleeping box and lots of things to play with. If it is allowed the run of the house, one must keep an eye on it, since it has a knack for vanishing and hiding in the oddest places.

Almost every pet store now sells a large, grotesque-looking bird with an enormous bill. This is the toucan from the tropical forests of America. There are about forty-one species of toucans; they vary in size, but most of them have brightly colored bills and plumage. The bill is usually as large as the entire body; this makes the toucan look top-heavy, and one wonders how it can keep its head up. Actually the bill is extremely light, almost hollow, a thin shell not more than one fiftieth to one thirtieth of an inch thick.

The toucan eats all kinds of fruits and berries, insects, some lizards, small snakes, and sometimes a mouse. It picks up a morsel of food very delicately with that clumsy-looking bill, tosses it into the air, and catches it in the open mouth. It gets very tame in captivity and is not hard to keep. But its odd way of feeding makes it very messy to have around the house. With a shake of the head, it will fling all excess or unwanted food for quite a distance against walls, ceiling, or the floor. Its feces are very loose, and the bird cannot be housebroken. The walls near it ought to be covered with plastic, and the floor lined with paper or absorbent material such as sawdust.

The toucan must have a roomy cage with natural branches

arranged so that the bird can hop up and down and horizontally. It is not a very strong flier, and hopping is its main way of locomotion. The branches should not be too close to the cage wire, so that it cannot break its bill against the wire. A toucan with a broken bill is unable to feed itself and must be fed by hand for the rest of its life.

The cage should not stand in direct sunlight since the toucan comes from the dense jungle where the sunlight is diffused. It is fond of bathing and of drinking water from a faucet. A shallow basin of lukewarm bath water should be given to it two or three times a week except in the winter, when once a week is often enough. (Of course it should have drinking water at all times.) Since it is so handy with its bill, the toucan can catch and toss light objects such as ping-pong balls, gloves, or sticks.

A smaller version of the toucan which is also frequently sold is the toucanet. Both should be cared for in the same way.

People who really want to show off their taste for exotic animals sometimes buy a young giant anteater. This animal belongs to the order of *Edentata,* which means "the toothless ones." But don't let the fact that the anteater has no teeth fool you into believing that it is therefore harmless. It has mean hooks, in the form of inwardly curved claws, on its forearms. It swings its arms freely when annoyed, and the claws can rip and tear an enemy savagely.

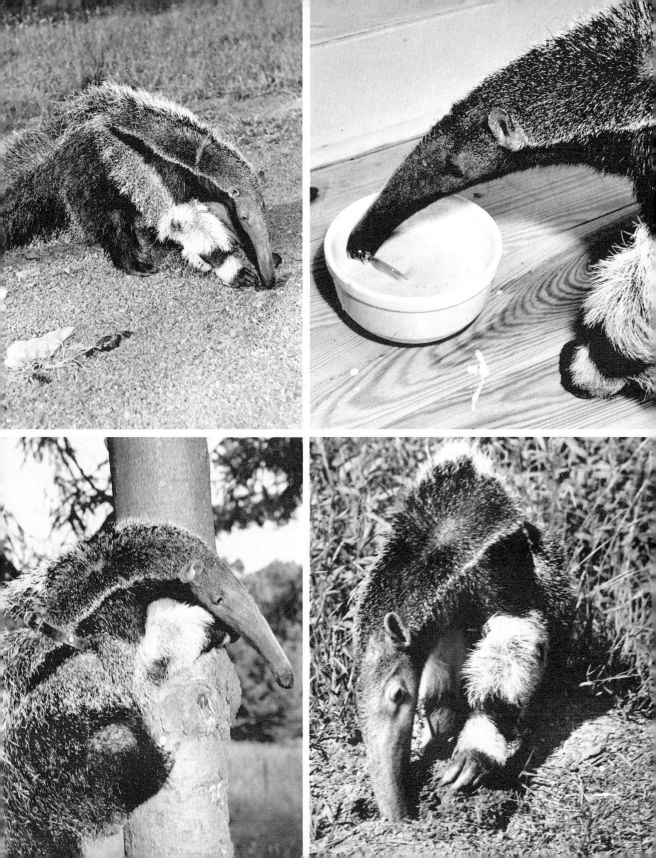

When young, the anteater is an amusing, friendly pet, but it is best kept outside in heated quarters. When grown, it weighs about fifty pounds, has long coarse hairs of white, gray, and black, and a bushy tail almost as long as the four-foot body. When asleep, the anteater covers itself with its tail. It has a long pointed muzzle and an almost twenty-inch wormlike, sticky tongue. The tongue is pushed into termite nests and then flicked back into the tiny mouth, with the termites and their eggs and larvae stuck to it. Termites seem to be the main food of the giant anteater, which is native from British Honduras south to northern Argentina. In captivity, it survives on a mixture of milk, raw eggs, lean chopped meat, pablum, a few drops of vitamins, and some cod-liver oil. It also likes to lap orange juice. The commercially dried ant eggs are shunned, but when led to an anthill it will dig into it and eat quite a few ants.

The giant anteater is basically a ground dweller, but it can climb if it wants to. Its walk is slow and shuffling, but when alarmed it moves with surprising speed. It is also a good swimmer. Naturally, its cage must be very strong and large. It should have a concrete floor because those sharp claws can rip through almost any wire bottom. Although the anteater is beautifully adapted to its natural environment, it is definitely not a pet that looks or feels at home in a household.

The list of exotic animals offered for sale goes on and on,

and every year new favorites are added. Only a few were discussed here. But before adopting or buying any strange pet, you should ask yourself these questions:

1. Are you really willing and able to make all the sacrifices necessary to care for an out-of-the-ordinary pet?
2. Do local laws allow the keeping of the animal?
3. Is the entire family willing to share in the care of the animal and the expense of feeding and housing it?
4. Will the animal remain tame after it is adult?
5. Can you provide a good substitute for the animal's natural life and habitat, so that it will not be just a prisoner in solitary confinement?
6. Are you willing to keep the animal for its entire life?
7. Is there no danger that the animal is threatened with extinction in its native land? (The Department of the Interior, Fish and Wildlife Service, in Washington, D.C., can supply a list.)

If all these questions can be answered in the affirmative, you might be the right kind of person to adopt a difficult pet.

A LISTING OF PROBLEM PETS